MARK McGWIRE
LEFTY GROVE
MIGUEL TEJADA
EDDIE COLLINS
RICKEY HENDERSON
JASON GIAMBI
DENNIS ECKERSLEY
JIMMIE FOXX
CATFISH HUNTER
TIM HUDSON
REGGIE JACKSON
DAVE STEWART

THE HISTORY OF THE
OAKLAND
ATHLETICS

AARON FRISCH

CREATIVE 🍎 EDUCATION

Published by Creative Education, 123 South Broad Street, Mankato, MN 56001

Creative Education is an imprint of The Creative Company.

Designed by Rita Marshall.

Photographs by AllSport (Otto Greule, Tom Hauck, Jed Jacobsohn), Associated Press/Wide World

Photos, Icon Sports Media (John Cordes), SportsChrome (Don Smith, Rob Tringali Jr., Michael Zito),

Sports Gallery (Al Messerschmidt)

Library of Congress Cataloging-in-Publication Data

Frisch, Aaron. The history of the Oakland Athletics / by Aaron Frisch.

p. cm. — (Baseball)   ISBN 1-58341-218-2

Summary: A team history of the "A's" born in Philadelphia, resident in Kansas City,

and now settled in Oakland, where for over thirty years they have been highly successful.

1. Oakland Athletics (Baseball team)—History—

Juvenile literature. [1. Oakland Athletics (Baseball team)—History.

2. Baseball—History.] I. Title. II. Baseball (Mankato, Minn.).

GV875.024 F75 2002   796.357'64'0979466—dc21   2001047879

First Edition 9 8 7 6 5 4 3 2 1

OAKLAND,

CALIFORNIA, IS NESTLED ALONG THE EASTERN SIDE OF

San Francisco Bay, just a few miles from San Francisco. Known as

the "Jewel of the East Bay" for its natural beauty, Oakland was born

in 1854 when gold prospectors drawn to the Bay Area founded a

new settlement. Since that time, Oakland has grown in the shadow **5**

of its bigger and more glamorous sister city across the bay.

When it comes to professional sports, however, Oakland takes

a back seat to no one. The city has long been home to football's

Raiders and basketball's Warriors, both successful franchises. Yet

even the accomplishments of those clubs pale in comparison to the

storied history of Oakland's baseball team, the Athletics. The Athletics,

commonly known as the A's, have loomed large in the American

CONNIE MACK

League (AL) for more than a century.

{THE PHILADELPHIA YEARS} The Athletics started out far

Frank "Home Run" Baker lived up to his name by leading the AL in homers from **1912** to **1914**.

from Oakland. In 1901, the Athletics were born as a charter member of the AL in Philadelphia, Pennsylvania. The driving force behind the team in those early days was Connie Mack, who owned and managed the club for 50 years. The Athletics quickly

6 became a powerhouse, winning the AL pennant four times between 1910 and 1914. Leading the way were a pair of hard-hitting infielders, third baseman Eddie Collins and second baseman Frank "Home Run" Baker.

Mack was a brilliant judge of baseball talent, but he was also tight-fisted with money. As a result, the Athletics had difficulty keeping star players, many of whom left Philadelphia behind to sign with other teams for bigger contracts. As they approached the

DENNIS ECKERSLEY

1920s, the A's sank in the standings as such standouts as pitchers Charles Albert "Chief" Bender and Eddie Plank moved on to greener pastures with other clubs.

But by the late 1920s, the Athletics were back with a vengeance. Philadelphia featured a slew of fine hitters during those years, including outfielder Al Simmons and catcher Mickey Cochrane. Also starring

Jimmie Foxx was a slugging marvel, averaging 27 home runs a season during his A's career.

for the A's was unbelievably strong first baseman Jimmie Foxx, who struck fear in the hearts of opposing pitchers with his monstrous home run blasts. "Foxx wasn't scouted," New York Yankees pitcher Lefty Gomez once quipped. "He was trapped."

With this great offense—and with superb pitching by Lefty Grove and George "Rube" Walberg—the powerful A's won the World Series in both 1929 and 1930. They won the AL pennant again in 1931 but fell short in their bid for a third world championship.

JIMMIE FOXX

The A's ruled the baseball world in the late **1920s** and again in the late '**80s**.

WALT WEISS

Then the team starting losing. First, it lost its star players to other teams again, then it fell into a losing slump that would last for two

The Athletics went through 10 different managers during their 13-season stay in Kansas City.

decades. By 1954, the A's were in such a sorry state that Philadelphia fans stopped coming to the park. So, looking for a fresh start, the team packed up and headed to Kansas City, Missouri.

{THE A'S MOVE WEST} Pitcher Bobby Shantz

12 and slugging outfielder Gus Zernial did their best to lead the A's up the standings in Kansas City, but their efforts went to waste as the team continued to lose. In 1960, the club was sold to a brash young businessman named Charles O. Finley. "Charlie O," as he was known, was wealthy, creative, and confident. Although players and managers sometimes found his personality overbearing, he would succeed in rebuilding the A's into a winner.

In the early 1960s, Finley made shrewd moves to bring in a

JIM HUNTER

number of talented players, including shortstop Bert Campaneris

and pitcher Jim Hunter. As he assembled the pieces of a quality team,

Finley also tried various means of drumming up media and fan interest

in the club. For example, when Hunter arrived in Kansas City, Finley

decided that the young pitcher needed a catchy nickname to grab

the attention of sportswriters. He dubbed the pitcher "Catfish" for no apparent reason, and the name stuck.

Finley continued bringing in talent throughout the mid-1960s.

In their inaugural season in Oakland, the A's posted their first winning mark (82–80) in 16 years. Among the new arrivals were outfielder Reggie Jackson, relief pitcher Rollie Fingers, and third baseman Sal Bando. By 1968, these players had the Athletics on the rise, but improvement didn't come fast enough for Kansas City fans. Due to poor attendance, the team packed up and headed west once more— this time to Oakland.

{FROM DROUGHT TO DYNASTY} The team's first season in Oakland was highlighted by the outstanding performance of Catfish Hunter. In 1968, the pitcher won Bay Area fans over by throwing the first regular-season perfect game (allowing no opposing players to reach base) in the AL in 46 years, mowing down the Minnesota Twins, one of the best hitting teams in the league. Off the mound,

REGGIE JACKSON

Hunter was also a key team leader who kept the club on an even keel with his calm personality.

The next season, Reggie Jackson was the big story in Oakland.

The charismatic young slugger clouted one home run after another that year, finishing with 47 round-trippers and becoming one of baseball's biggest attractions. "When you hit a terrific shot, all the players come to rest at that moment and watch you," Jackson

explained. "Everyone is helpless and in awe. You charge people up

by hitting the long ball."

In 1971, the A's put it all together. Under new

manager Dick Williams, the team soared to the top of

the AL Western Division (the league was split into

two divisions in 1969) with a 101–60 record. Leading

the charge was young pitcher Vida Blue, who enjoyed a dream season

with 24 wins and a tiny 1.82 ERA—numbers that earned him both

the AL Cy Young Award as the league's best pitcher and the AL Most

Valuable Player (MVP) award.

Oakland fell short of the World Series in 1971, but it would

not be denied the next season. After winning its division again in

1972, the team blazed past the Detroit Tigers in the AL

Championship Series to reach the World Series for the first time in

Pitcher Vida Blue struck out almost eight batters per game during his incredible **1971** season.

VIDA BLUE

The A's have played in Network Associates Coliseum ever since moving to Oakland.

41 years. Most experts gave Oakland little chance of beating

Cincinnati and its powerful "Big Red Machine" lineup of Johnny

The power of outfielder Jose Canseco helped make up for the loss of Reggie Jackson in the **'80s**.

Bench, Joe Morgan, and Pete Rose. The A's weren't

intimidated, however, and shocked the baseball world

by beating the Reds in seven games to capture the

world title.

But Oakland was just getting warmed up. The A's

20 came back to win the World Series again in both 1973 and 1974.

Jackson led the team past the New York Mets in 1973, and Rollie

Fingers dominated the Los Angeles Dodgers in 1974. In beating the

Dodgers, the A's became just the second team in major-league

history to win three straight world championships.

{REBUILDING IN THE BAY} Oakland and its fans were on

top of the world in the mid-1970s, but the winds of change started

blowing. In a bitter replay of the A's early history, the team began to

JOSE CANSECO

lose all of its star players. Unable or unwilling to pay big contracts,

Finley sold off the pieces of his dynasty, including the popular

Reggie Jackson. Drained of talent, the A's plummeted to the bottom

of the standings.

In 1980, Billy Martin was brought in as the team's new manager.

Martin was known for his fiery, no-nonsense personality and

worked his players hard. Under his guidance, the A's began to turn things around. One of the players most responsible for the improvement was young outfielder Rickey Henderson, whose blazing speed and unwavering confidence made him perhaps the greatest base-stealer of all time. In 1982, Henderson set a new major-league record with an incredible 130 steals.

Fiery pitcher Dave Stewart spent eight seasons with Oakland, averaging almost 15 wins a year.

Martin stepped down as manager before the 1983 season, and the team slipped in the standings until Tony La Russa came on board as the new manager in 1986. La Russa knew Oakland had talent, but he felt it needed some team leaders. The manager soon found one of those leaders in pitcher Dave Stewart.

Stewart was known for his hot temper, but La Russa gradually helped him channel his emotions into better pitching. With an intimidating glare and a wicked forkball (a pitch like a fastball that

DAVE STEWART

The amazingly fast Rickey Henderson swiped 100 or more bases in three seasons.

RICKEY HENDERSON

sinks when it reaches the plate), Stewart won 20 games in 1987, a

feat he would repeat the next three seasons. "Dave uses the same

energy that used to hurt him—anger—to now help

him concentrate and focus," explained A's pitching

coach Dave Duncan. "Where before he was all over

the place emotionally, now he's all business."

The A's were also intimidating at the plate in

Prolific power-
hitting first
baseman Mark
McGwire
represented
Oakland in
nine All-Star
Games.

1987. The most daunting hitter was first baseman Mark McGwire,   **25**

who set a major-league rookie record by slamming 49 home runs. A

year later, it was Jose Canseco's turn to shine. That season, the strap-

ping young outfielder led the AL with 42 home runs and stole 40

bases, becoming the first big-league player in the "40–40" club—a

feat that earned him the AL MVP award.

The "Bash Brothers," as McGwire and Canseco were known,

helped Oakland reach the World Series in 1988. The A's lost that

MARK McGWIRE

series to a powerful Los Angeles Dodgers team, but they returned to

the Fall Classic again the next year, this time to face their rivals from

across the Bay—the San Francisco Giants. Not even an earthquake

that rocked the Bay Area in game three and delayed the World Series

for a week could stop the A's. With the help of designated hitter

Dave Parker and reliever Dennis Eckersley, Oakland cruised to the championship in four straight games.

The A's nearly repeated as champs in 1990. Pitcher Bob Welch won 27 games—the most in the majors in 22 years—and Stewart won another 22 as Oakland rolled to a 103–59 record. The A's then advanced to the World Series, where many experts expected them to crush the Cincinnati Reds. Instead, the Reds toppled the mighty A's in a stunning four-game sweep.

With his mighty swing and great leadership, Jason Giambi led the young A's back to prominence.

{THE END OF A CENTURY} After the A's posted strong records but missed the World Series in 1991 and 1992, the team's roster changed dramatically. Canseco, Stewart, Henderson, shortstop Walt Weiss, and other stars were either traded or released as Oakland rebuilt with younger players. In 1995, Tony La Russa decided to move on as well, ending his 10-year reign as Oakland's manager.

The A's suffered numerous setbacks in the late 1990s. For

JASON GIAMBI

instance, Oakland fans were thrilled in 1997 when Canseco returned to the A's and was reunited with his "Bash Brother" Mark McGwire.

In **1998**, outfielder Ben Grieve became the fifth A's player to earn AL Rookie of the Year honors.

But Canseco spent much of the time on the bench with nagging injuries, and Oakland management— fearing that McGwire would soon leave the team as a free agent—traded the longtime first baseman to the St. Louis Cardinals.

Over the next few seasons, the team brought in a number of promising young players in an attempt to rebuild. These included third baseman Eric Chavez, shortstop Miguel Tejada, outfielder Ben Grieve, and slugging first baseman Jason Giambi. Under the patient guidance of new manager Art Howe, the young A's showed steady improvement. Oakland clawed its way back up the standings, going 91–70 in 2000 and making the playoffs for the first of two straight seasons.

BEN GRIEVE

Leading Oakland's resurgence was the free-spirited and hard-

hitting Giambi, who arrived as a true superstar in 2000. That season,

he batted .333, jacked 43 home runs, and drove in

137 runs—numbers that earned him the AL MVP

award. Playing an equally prominent role in Oakland's

success, however, was the team's talented young

pitching staff, led by Tim Hudson, Barry Zito, and

Mark Mulder.

Rising star
Miguel Tejada
drove in 115
runs in **2000**,
more than
any other
shortstop in
club history.

The A's fell to the New York Yankees in the divisional playoffs

in both 2000 and 2001, but the team had rightly reclaimed its status

as a force in the AL. Unfortunately, the A's were then dealt another

tough blow when Giambi left the team for a bigger contract with

the Yankees. But with a lineup comprised mainly of quality players

in their mid-20s, Oakland believed that it could still challenge for a

championship. "Everyone is going to have to step up their game, not

MIGUEL TEJADA

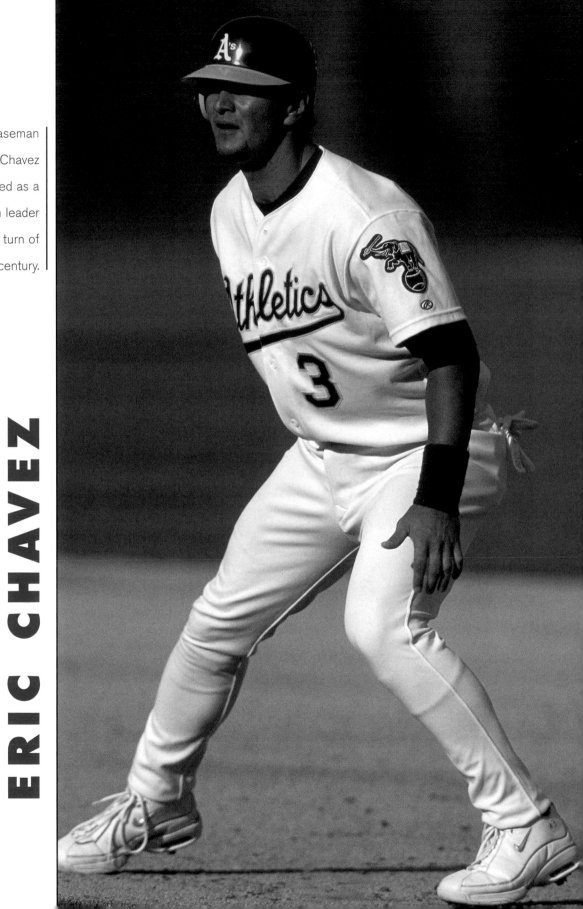

Third baseman
Eric Chavez
emerged as a
team leader
at the turn of
the century.

ERIC CHAVEZ

Pitcher Mark
Mulder rose to
stardom in
2001, ending
the year with a
21–8 record.

MARK MULDER

out of pressure but out of necessity," said Chavez after Giambi's

departure. "[We] have a good team on paper, but if we want to

compete, we have to grow up fast."

Fans hoped
that young
gun Tim
Hudson would
help Oakland
charge to
its 10th
world title.

The A's franchise turned 100 years old in 2001, and

what a century it was. Including the team's history in

Philadelphia and Kansas City, the Athletics captured

15 AL pennants and nine world championships to

rank among the most dominant teams of all time. As they continue

to swing for the fences, today's A's plan to add to those totals and

make Oakland the jewel of the baseball world once again.

TIM HUDSON